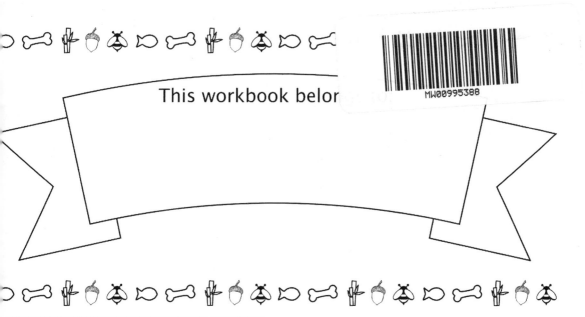

This workbook belor

Hello 你好 nǐ hǎo

This workbook is for practicing to write Chinese characters. Pinyin, English translations and pictures are used to describe the characters. Write two pages at least two times a week. Think about the pronounciation, meaning and stroke order of each character while writing.

Trace over the gray characters by following the correct numbered stroke order as shown for the first few grids. Do not worry about the thickness of the gray lines. Use a pencil or pen to trace down the middle of the gray lines. Practice with the 2 sample grids below.

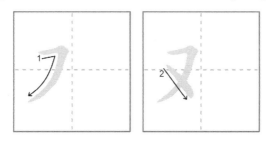

Thank you for choosing **Chinese For Kids 50 More Characters Ages 5+ (Simplified)**. Have fun writing and learning!

Chinese For Kids 50 More Characters Ages 5+ (Simplified)

ISBN-13: 978-1720475743
ISBN-10: 1720475741

© 2018 Queenie Law
Adore Neko Designs (www.adoreneko.com)

kāi
open

开

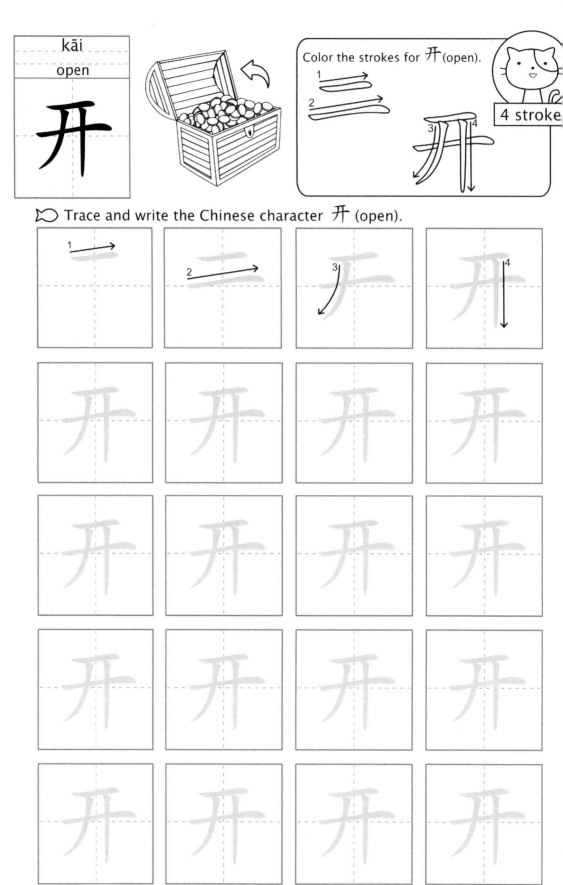

Color the strokes for 开 (open).

1
2
3 4

4 strokes

Trace and write the Chinese character 开 (open).

Write the missing stroke for 开 on each open chest from the fish 鱼 to the cat 猫.

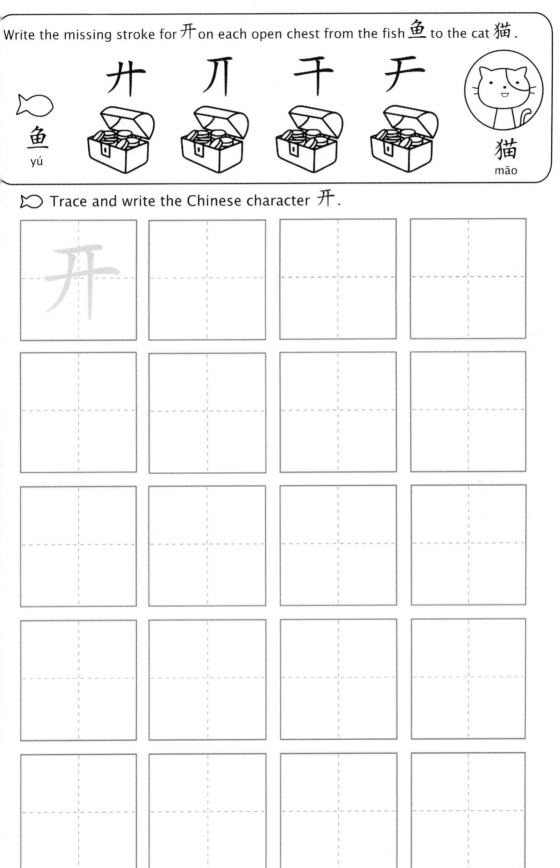

鱼
yú

卅　刀　干　亍

猫
māo

Trace and write the Chinese character 开.

guān

close

关

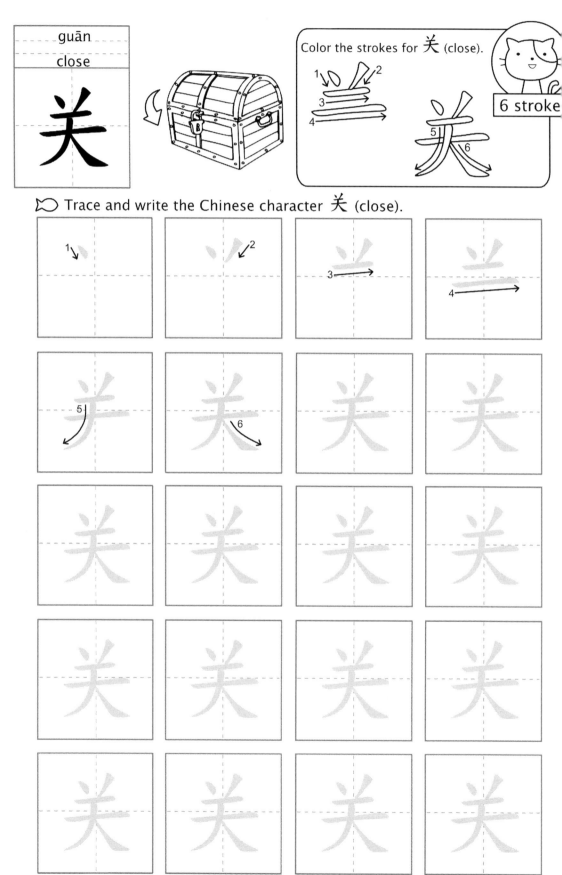

Color the strokes for 关 (close).

6 stroke

🐟 Trace and write the Chinese character 关 (close).

Write the missing stroke for 关 on each closed chest from the fish 鱼 to the cat 猫.

夫 夫 关 关 丷 羊

鱼
yú

猫
māo

Trace and write the Chinese character 关.

duō

many

多

Color the strokes for 多 (many).

6 stroke

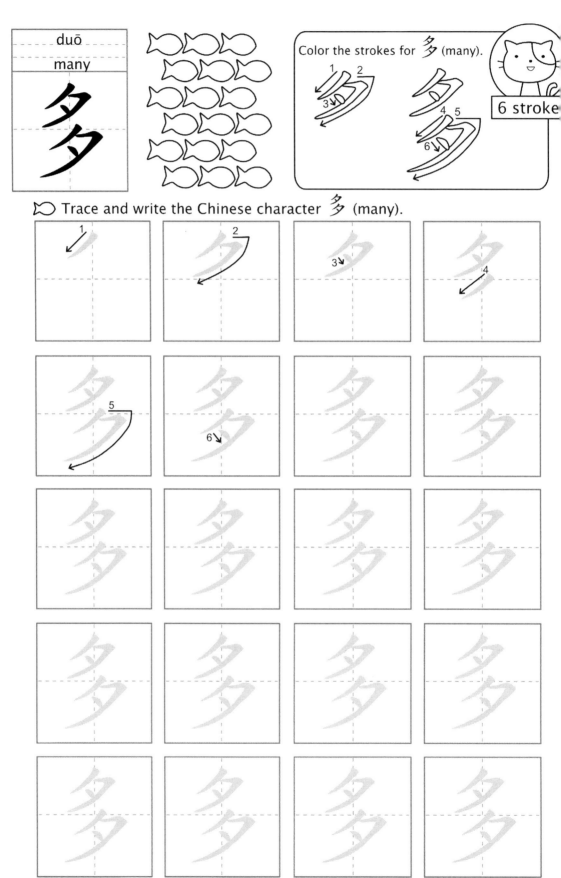

Trace and write the Chinese character 多 (many).

Write the missing stroke for 多 from the fish 鱼 to the cat 猫.

鱼
yú

猫
māo

🐟 Trace and write the Chinese character 多 .

shǎo

few

少

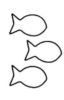

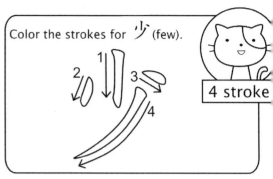

Trace and write the Chinese character 少 (few).

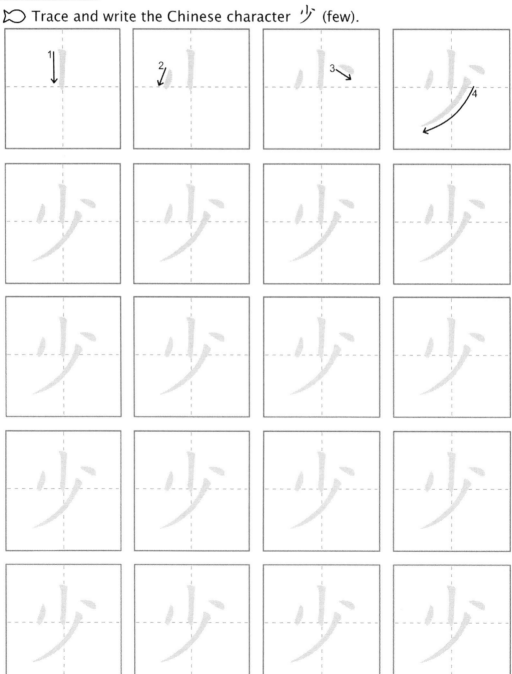

Write the missing stroke for 少 from the fish 鱼 to the cat 猫.

鱼
yú

猫
māo

Trace and write the Chinese character 少.

zhǐ

stop

止

STOP

Color the strokes for 止 (stop).

4 stroke

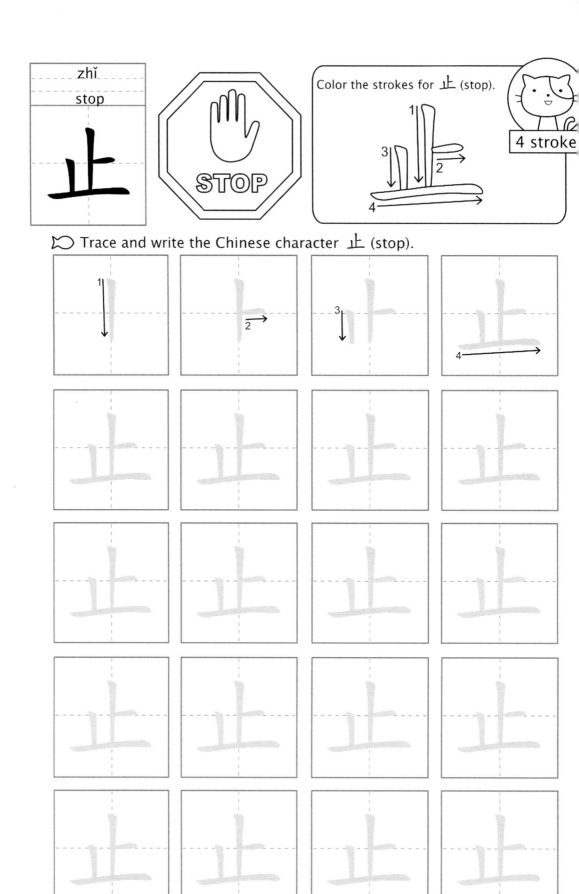

Trace and write the Chinese character 止 (stop).

Write the missing stroke for 止 in each stop sign from the cat 猫 to the fish 鱼.

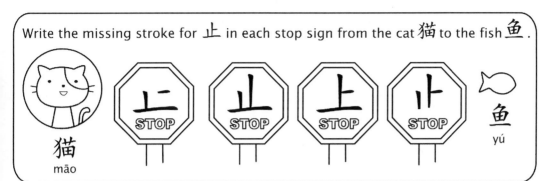

猫
māo

鱼
yú

Trace and write the Chinese character 止.

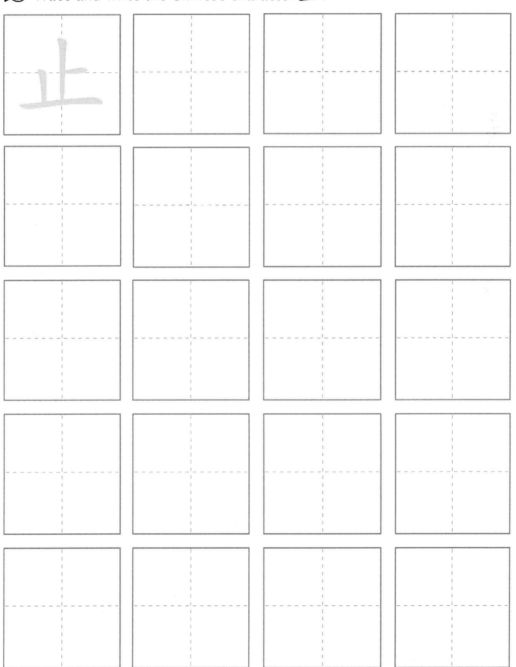

qù

go

去

GO

Color the strokes for 去 (go).

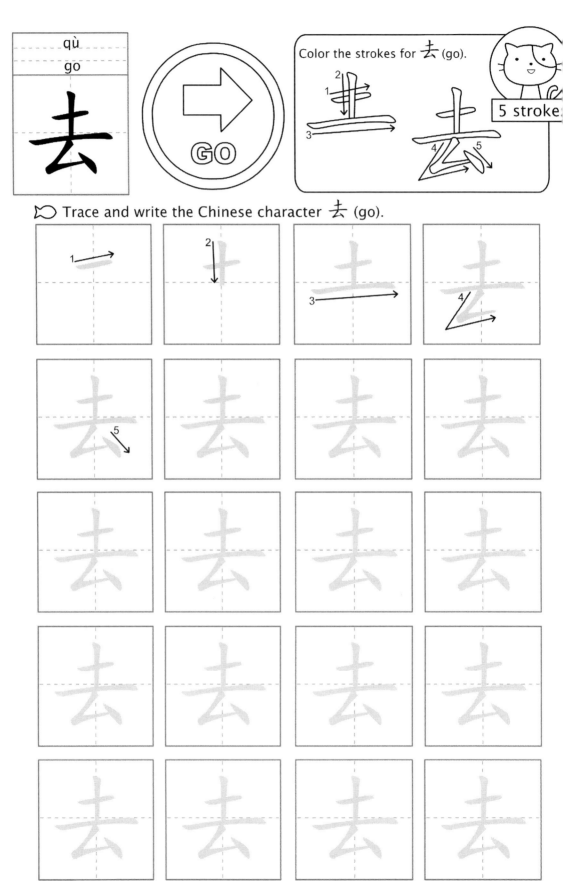

5 strokes

🐟 Trace and write the Chinese character 去 (go).

Write the missing stroke for 去 in each go sign from the cat 猫 to the fish 鱼.

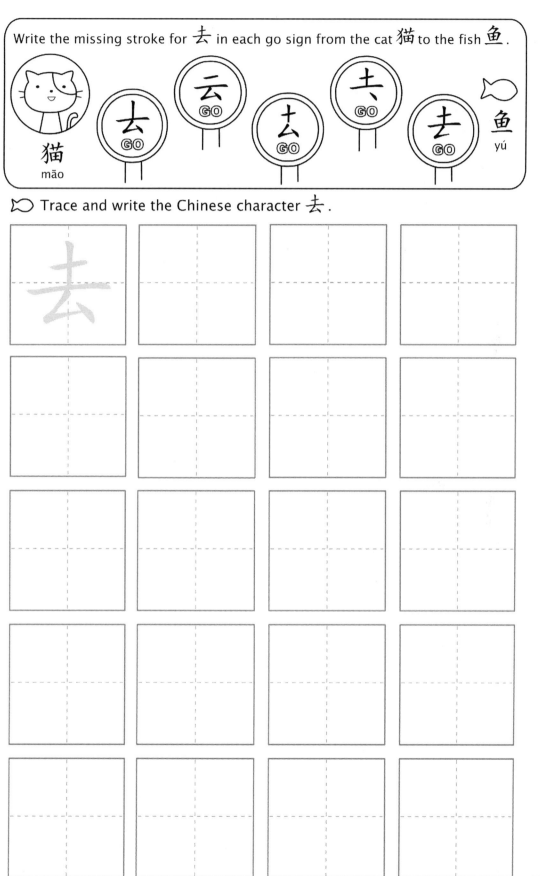

猫
māo

云
GO

去
GO

厶
GO

土
GO

去
GO

鱼
yú

Trace and write the Chinese character 去.

zuǒ

left

左

Color the strokes for 左 (left).

5 stroke

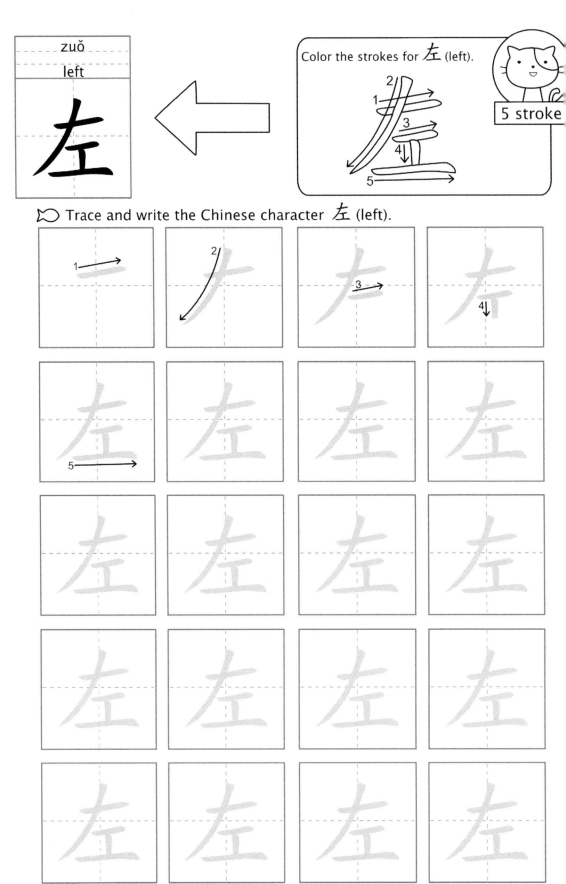

Trace and write the Chinese character 左 (left).

Write the missing stroke for 左 in each left arrow from the cat 猫 to the fish 鱼.

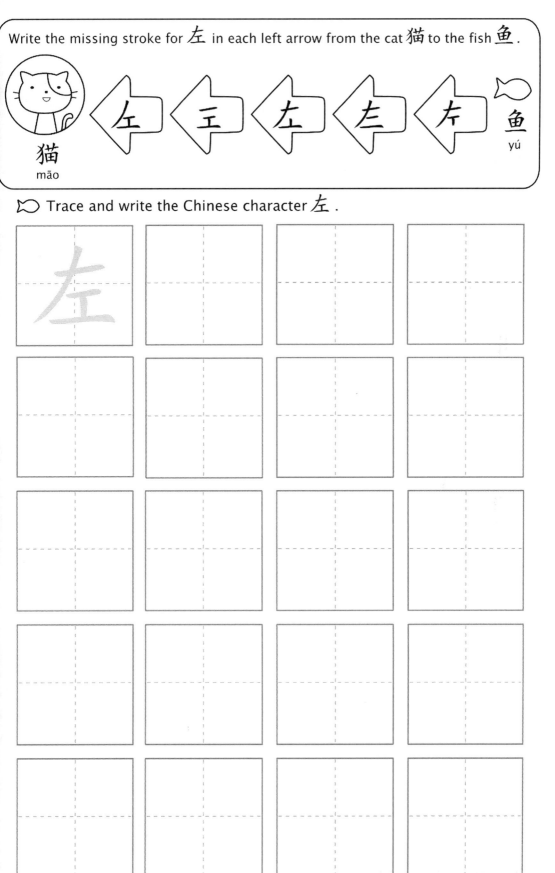

猫
māo

鱼
yú

🐟 Trace and write the Chinese character 左 .

yòu

right

右

Color the strokes for 右 (right).

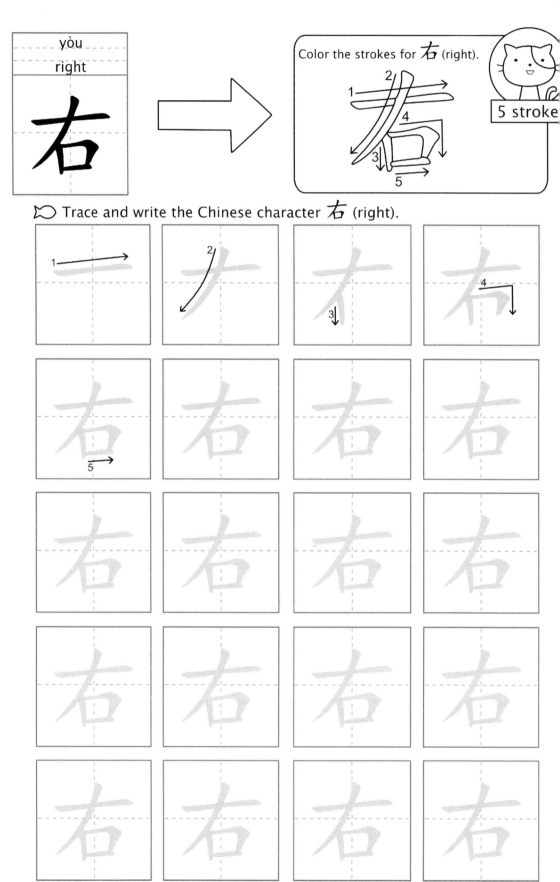

5 stroke

Trace and write the Chinese character 右 (right).

Write the missing stroke for 右 in each right arrow from the cat 猫 to the fish 鱼.

Trace and write the Chinese character 右.

nèi

inside

内

Color the strokes for 内 (inside).

4 stroke

🐟 Trace and write the Chinese character 内 (inside).

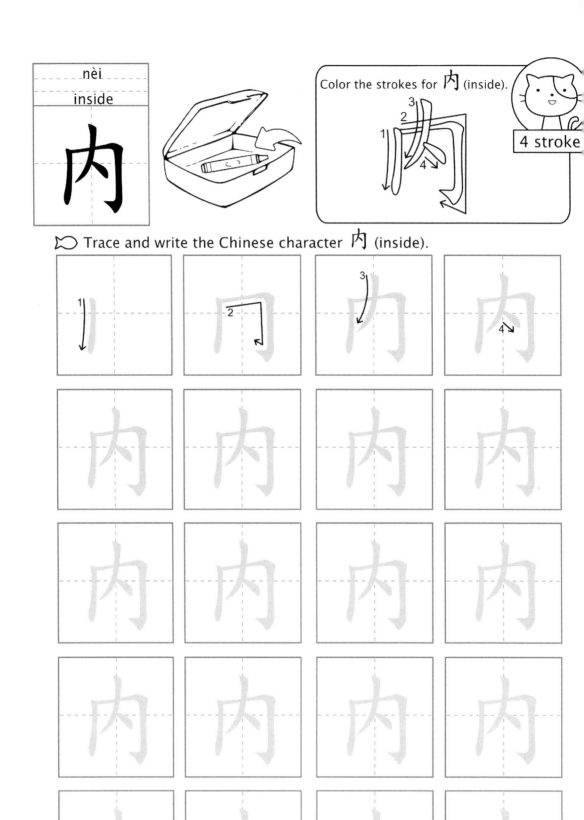

Write the missing stroke for 内 in each frame from the cat 猫 to the fish 鱼.

猫
māo

勹　人　冂　内

鱼
yú

🐟 Trace and write the Chinese character 内.

内

wài

outside

外

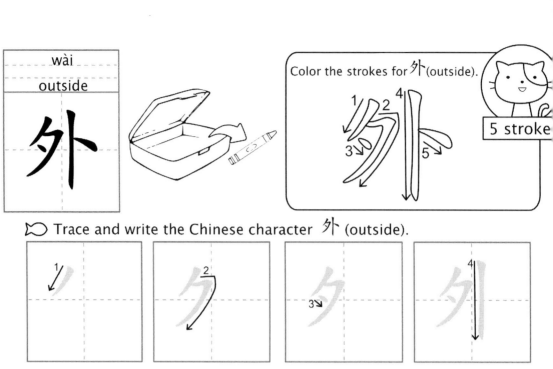

Color the strokes for 外 (outside).

5 stroke

🐟 Trace and write the Chinese character 外 (outside).

20

Write the missing stroke for 外 outside each box from the cat 猫 to the fish 鱼.

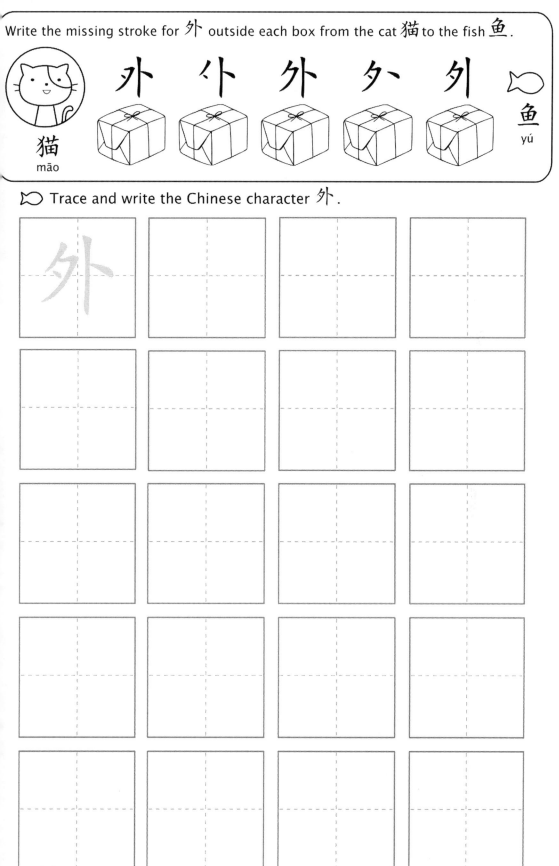

外　卜　外　夕　列

猫
māo

鱼
yú

Trace and write the Chinese character 外.

外

Good Job!

Practice writing characters you have learned below.

Good Job! Practice writing characters you have learned below.

niú

cow

牛

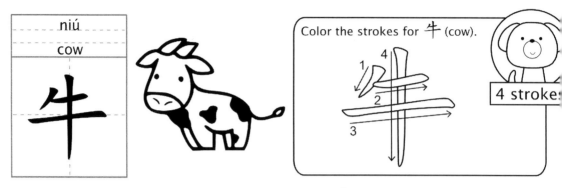

Color the strokes for 牛 (cow).

4 strokes

Trace and write the Chinese character 牛 (cow).

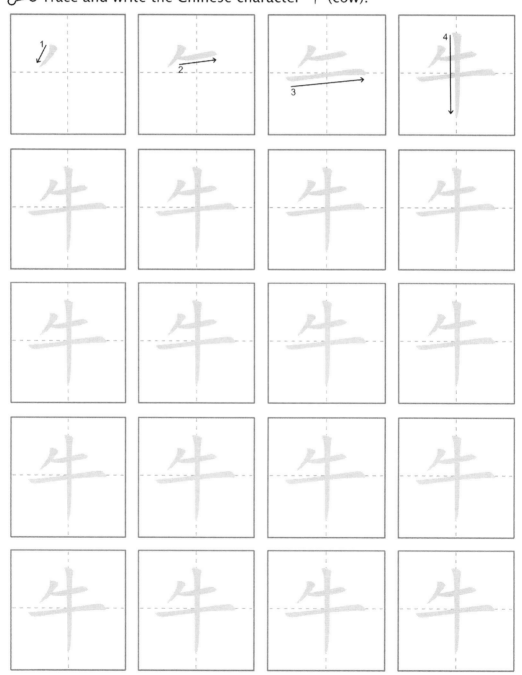

Write the missing stroke for 牛 on each cow from the dog 狗 to the bone 骨.

丰　牛　牜　二

狗
gǒu

骨
gǔ

🦴 Trace and write the Chinese character 牛.

yáng

sheep

羊

Color the strokes for 羊 (sheep).

6 strokes

Trace and write the Chinese character 羊 (sheep).

Write the missing stroke for 羊 on each sheep from the dog 狗 to the bone 骨.

羊　羊　羊　羊　羊　兰

狗
gǒu

骨
gǔ

Trace and write the Chinese character 羊.

羊

mǎ

horse

马

Color the strokes for 马 (horse).

3 strokes

Trace and write the Chinese character 马 (horse).

Write the missing stroke for 马 on each horse from the dog 狗 to the bone 骨.

Trace and write the Chinese character 马.

niǎo

bird

鸟

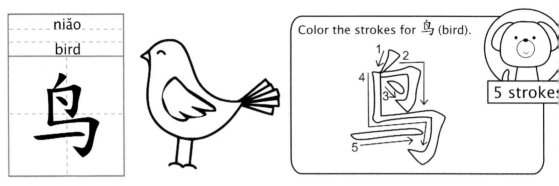

Color the strokes for 鸟 (bird).

5 strokes

🦴 Trace and write the Chinese character 鸟 (bird).

Write the missing stroke for 鸟 on each bowl from the dog 狗 to the bone 骨.

狗
gǒu

鸟　　乌　　乌　　乌　　鸟　　骨
gǔ

Trace and write the Chinese character 鸟 .

jī

chicken

鸡

Color the strokes for 鸡 (chicken).

7 strokes

🦴 Trace and write the Chinese character 鸡 (chicken).

Write the missing stroke for 鸡 on each chicken from the dog 狗 to the bone 骨.

狗
gǒu

鸟 鸡 鸡 鸡 鸡 鸡 鸡

骨
gǔ

Trace and write the Chinese character 鸡.

鸡

tián

field

田

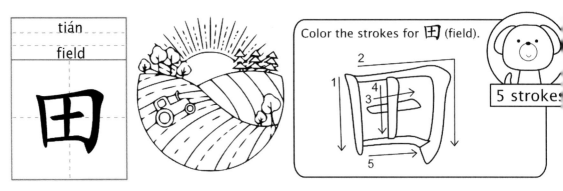

Color the strokes for 田 (field).

5 strokes

Trace and write the Chinese character 田 (field).

Write the missing stroke for 田 on each field from the dog 狗 to the bone 骨.

🦴 Trace and write the Chinese character 田.

chí
pond

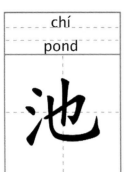

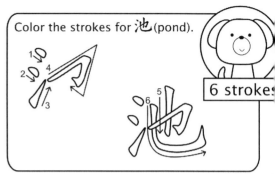

6 strokes

🦴 Trace and write the Chinese character 池 (pond).

Write the missing stroke for 池 in each pond from the dog 狗 to the bone 骨.

狗
gǒu

池 池 池 氾 氾

池 氿 汕

骨
gǔ

Trace and write the Chinese character 池.

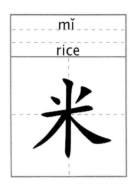

mǐ

rice

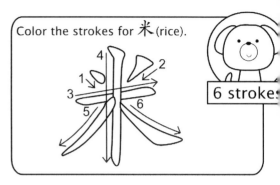

Color the strokes for 米 (rice).

6 strokes

🦴 Trace and write the Chinese character 米 (rice).

Write the missing stroke for 米 on each grain of rice from the dog 狗 to the bone 骨.

狗
gǒu

米 米 米 关 半 半

骨
gǔ

Trace and write the Chinese character 米.

guā

melon

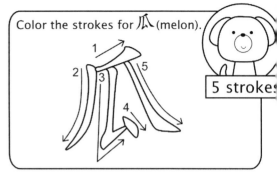

Color the strokes for 瓜 (melon).

5 strokes

Trace and write the Chinese character 瓜 (melon).

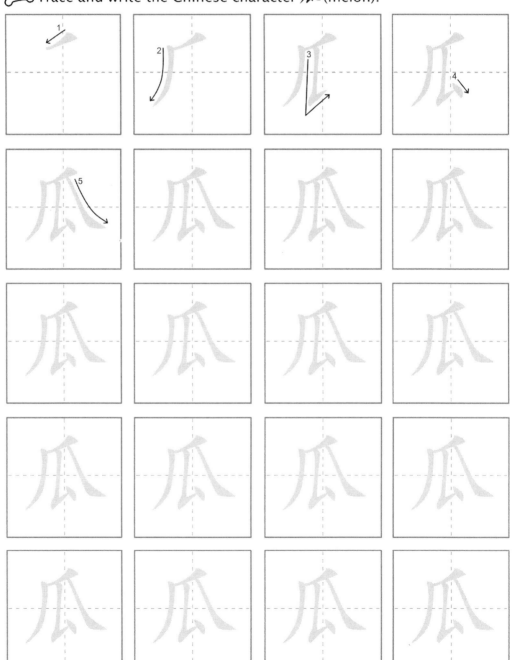

Write the missing stroke for 瓜 on each melon from the dog 狗 to the bone 骨.

瓜 瓜 瓜 瓜 瓜

狗
gǒu

骨
gǔ

Trace and write the Chinese character 瓜.

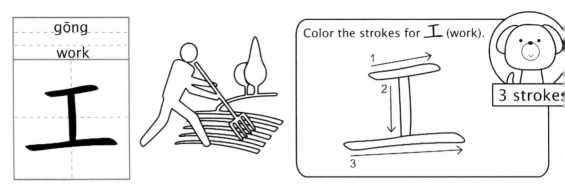

gōng

work

工

Color the strokes for 工 (work).

3 strokes

🦴 Trace and write the Chinese character 工 (work).

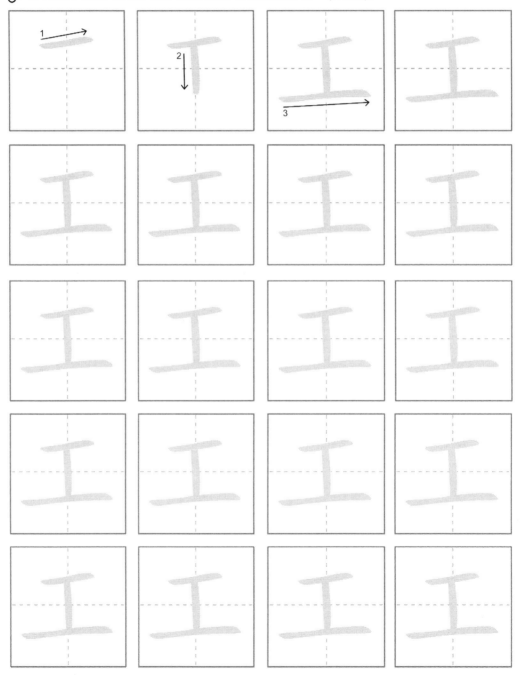

Write the missing stroke for 工 on each worker from the dog 狗 to the bone 骨.

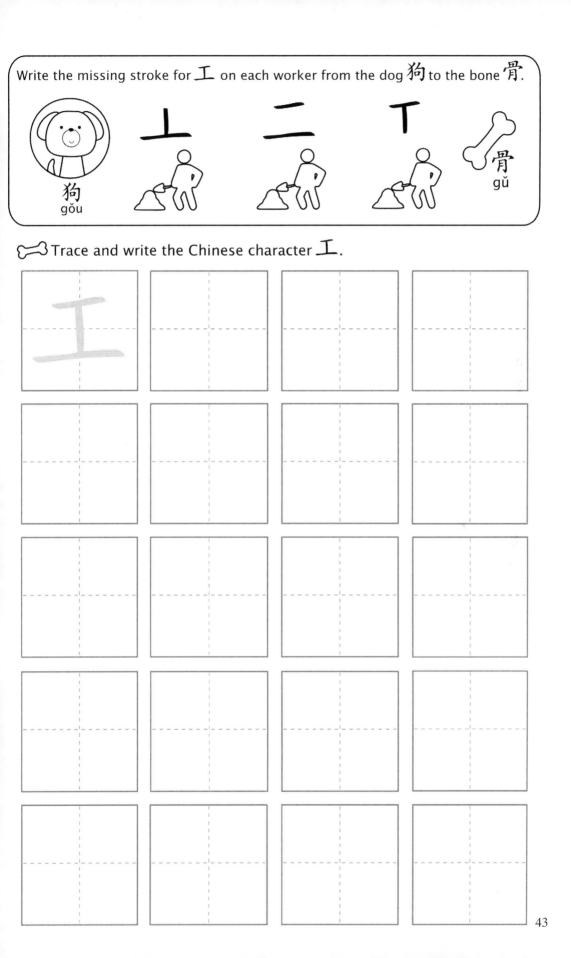

狗
gǒu

骨
gǔ

Trace and write the Chinese character 工.

Good Job! Practice writing characters you have learned below.

Good Job! Practice writing characters you have learned below.

bǎi

hundred

百

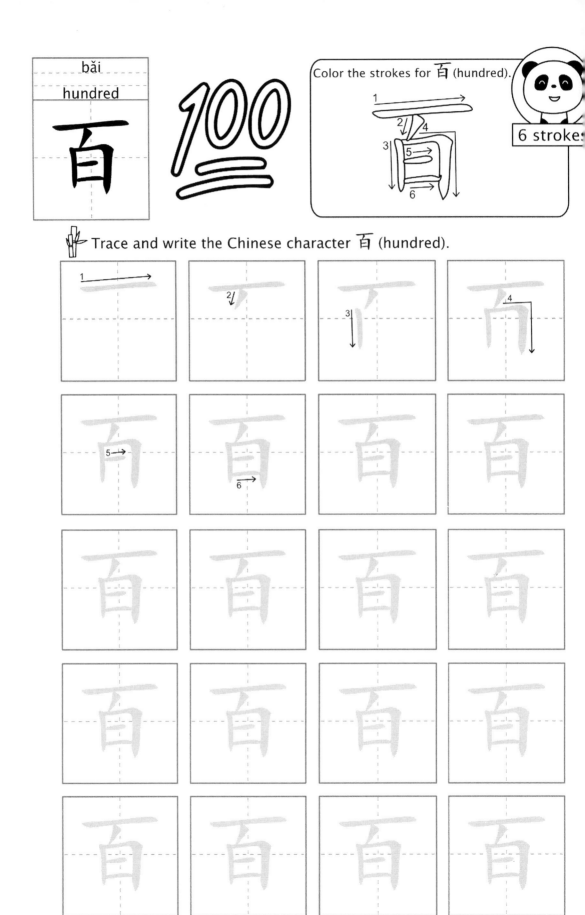

Color the strokes for 百 (hundred).

6 strokes

Trace and write the Chinese character 百 (hundred).

Write the missing stroke for 百 on each hundred from the panda 熊猫 to the bamboo 竹子.

白　百　百　百　百　百

(100) (100) (100) (100) (100) (100)

熊猫
xióngmāo

竹子
zhúzi

Trace and write the Chinese character 百.

百

qiān

thousand

千 1000

Color the strokes for 千 (thousand).

3 strokes

Trace and write the Chinese character 千 (thousand).

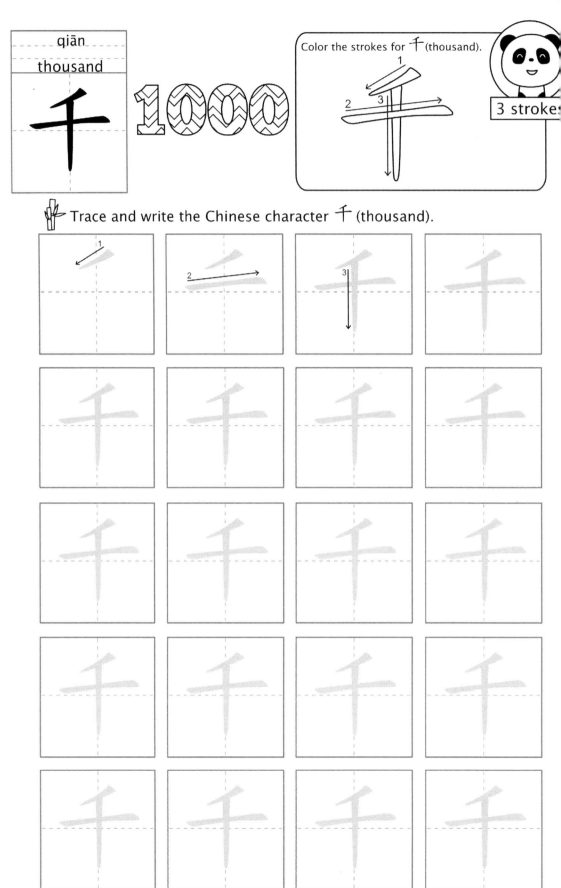

Write the missing stroke for 千 on each thousand from the panda 熊猫 to the bamboo 竹子.

Trace and write the Chinese character 千.

dāo

knife

刀

Color the strokes for 刀 (knife).

2 strokes

Trace and write the Chinese character 刀 (knife).

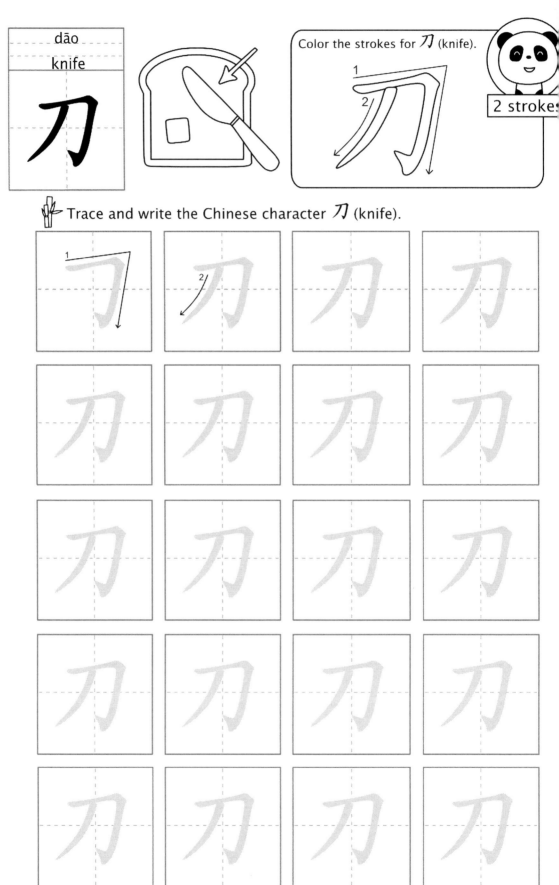

Write the missing stroke for 刀 on each knife from the panda 熊猫 to the bamboo 竹子.

熊猫
xióngmāo

竹子
zhúzi

Trace and write the Chinese character 刀.

qiè
cut

切

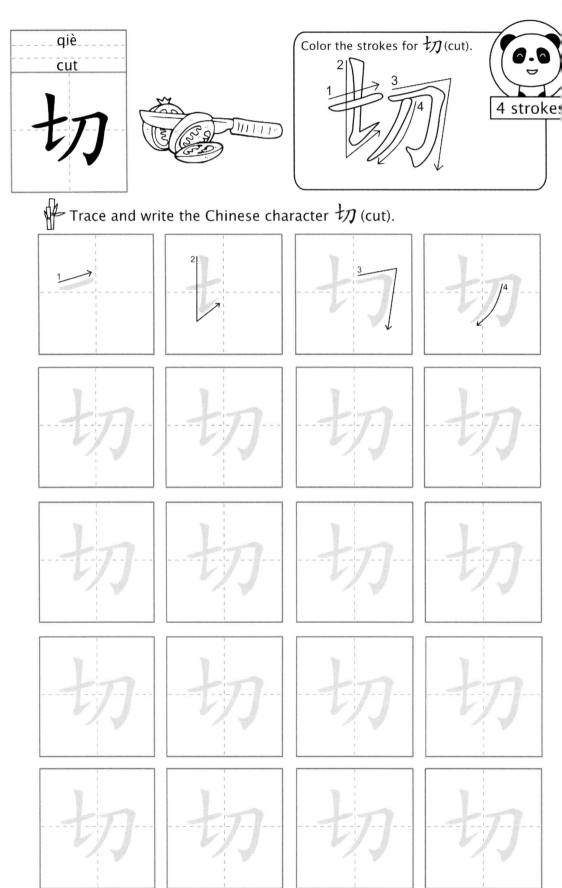

Color the strokes for 切 (cut).

4 strokes

Trace and write the Chinese character 切 (cut).

Write the missing stroke for 切 on the cutting pictures from the panda 熊猫 to the bamboo 竹子.

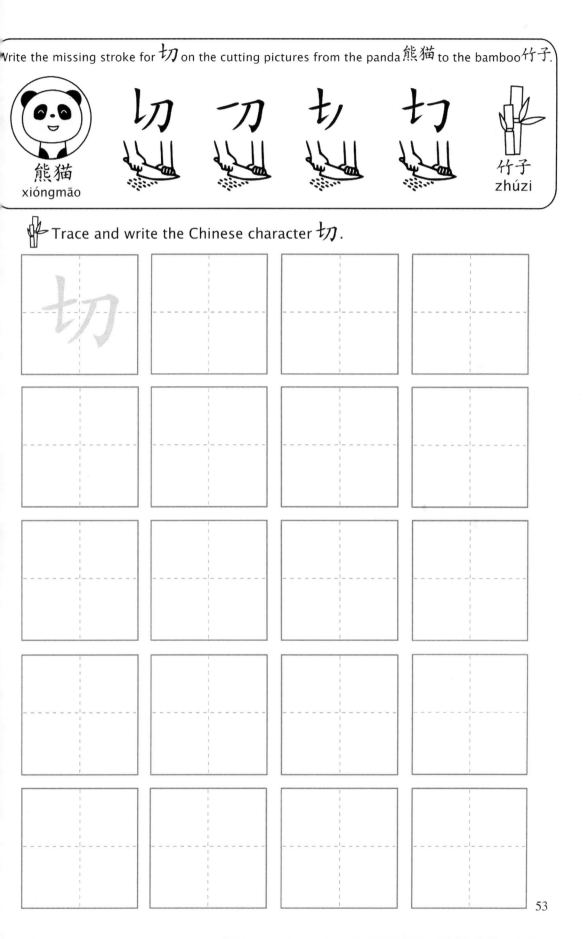

熊猫
xióngmāo

切　刀　切　切

竹子
zhúzi

Trace and write the Chinese character 切.

xiě
write

写

write

Color the strokes for 写 (write).

5 strokes

Trace and write the Chinese character 写 (write).

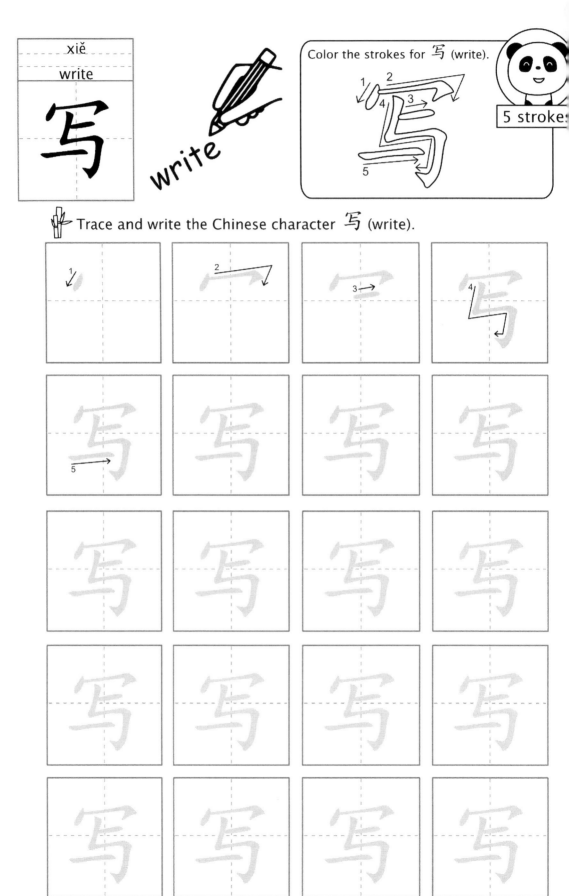

Write the missing stroke for 写 in each note from the panda 熊猫 to the bamboo 竹子.

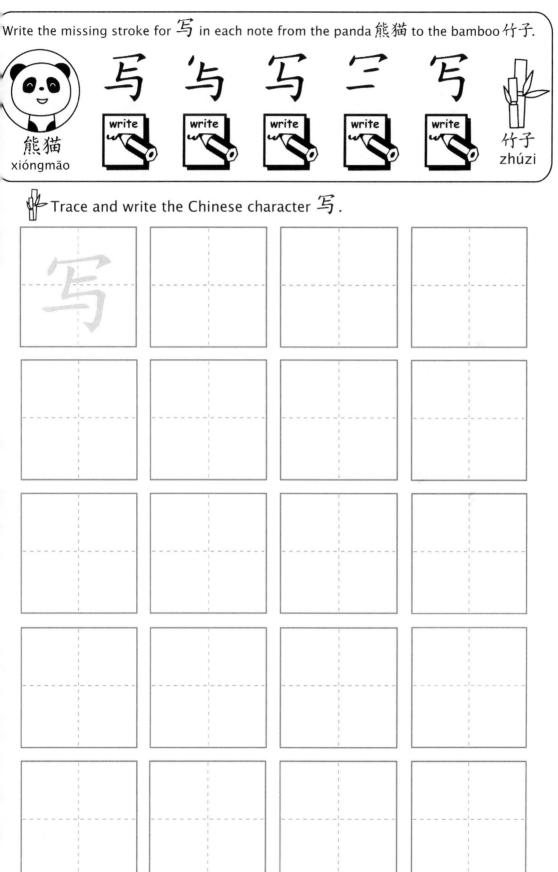

熊猫
xióngmāo

写　与　写　二　写

write　write　write　write　write

竹子
zhúzi

Trace and write the Chinese character 写.

zì

word

字

WORD

Trace and write the Chinese character 字 (word).

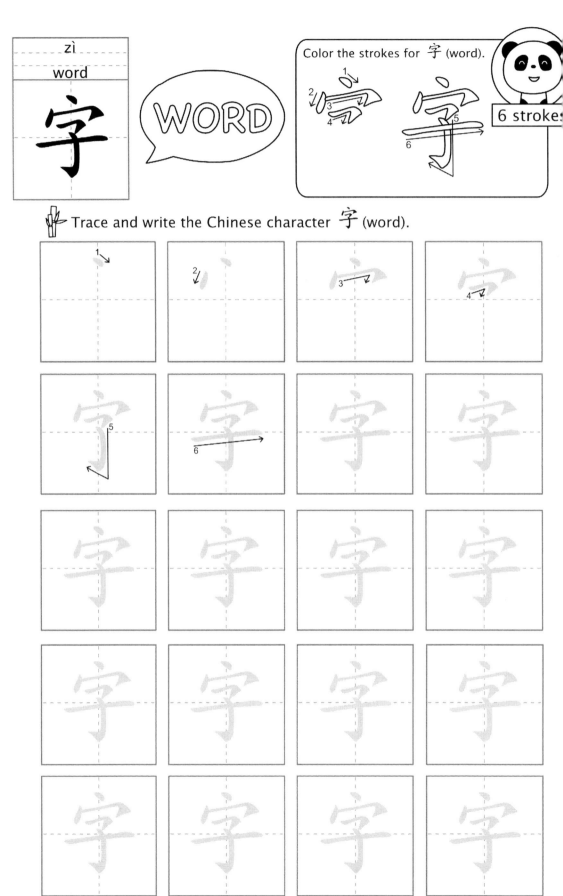

Write the missing stroke for 字 in each bubble from the panda 熊猫 to the bamboo 竹子.

熊猫
xióngmāo

竹子
zhúzi

Trace and write the Chinese character 字.

sè

color

色

COLOR

Color the strokes for 色 (color).

6 strokes

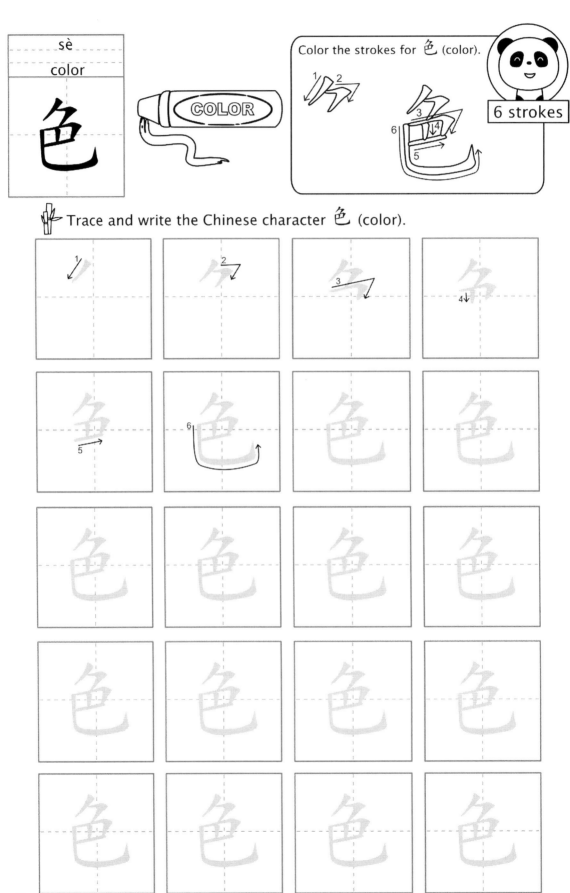

Trace and write the Chinese character 色 (color).

Write the missing strokes for 色 each crayon from the panda 熊猫 to the bamboo 竹子.

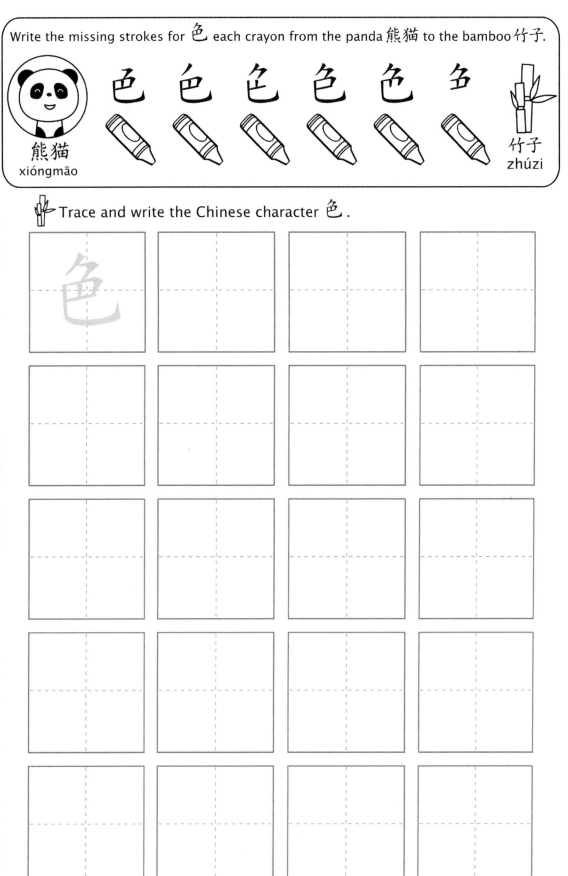

熊猫
xióngmāo

竹子
zhúzi

Trace and write the Chinese character 色 .

hóng
red

红

RED

Trace and write the Chinese character 红 (red).

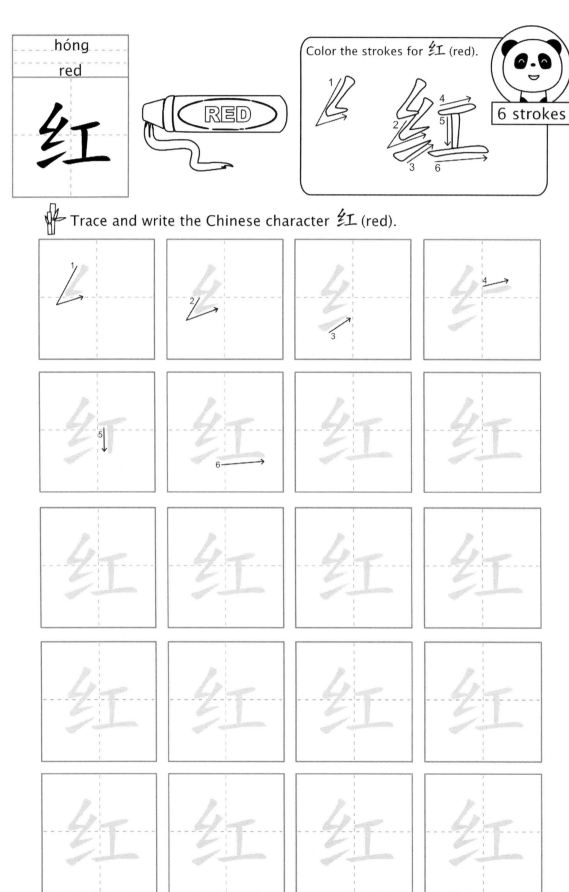

Write the missing stroke for 红 on each crayon from the panda 熊猫 to the bamboo 竹子.

红 红 红 红 纟 红

熊猫
xióngmāo

竹子
zhúzi

Trace and write the Chinese character 红.

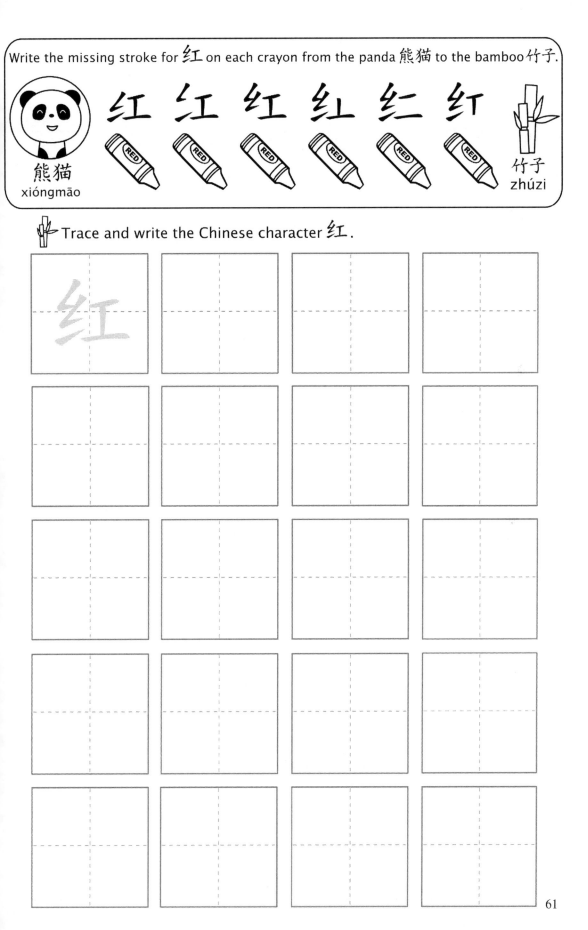

bái

white

白

WHITE

Color the strokes for 白 (white).

5 strokes

Trace and write the Chinese character 白 (white).

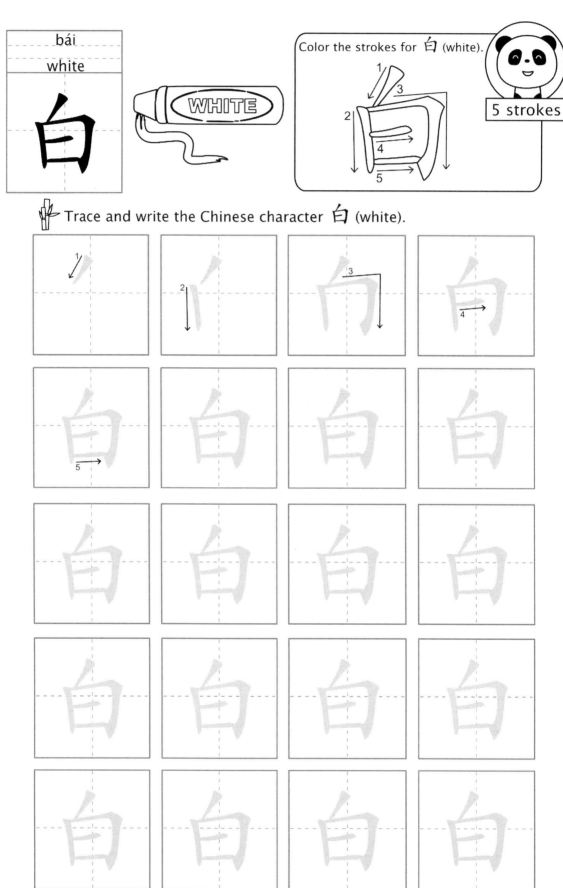

Write the missing stroke for 白 on each crayon from the panda 熊猫 to the bamboo 竹子.

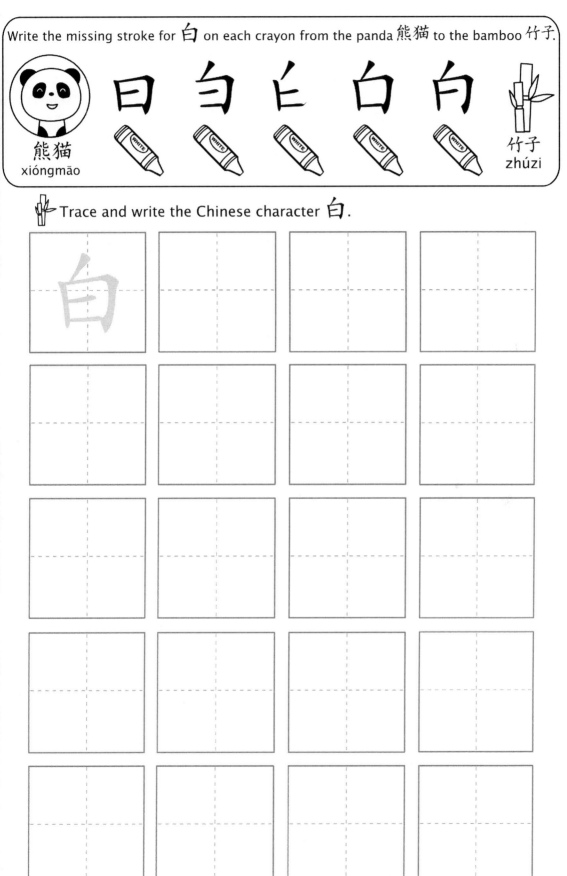

熊猫
xióngmāo

竹子
zhúzi

Trace and write the Chinese character 白.

huī

gray

灰

GRAY

Color the strokes for 灰 (gray).

6 strokes

Trace and write the Chinese character 灰 (gray).

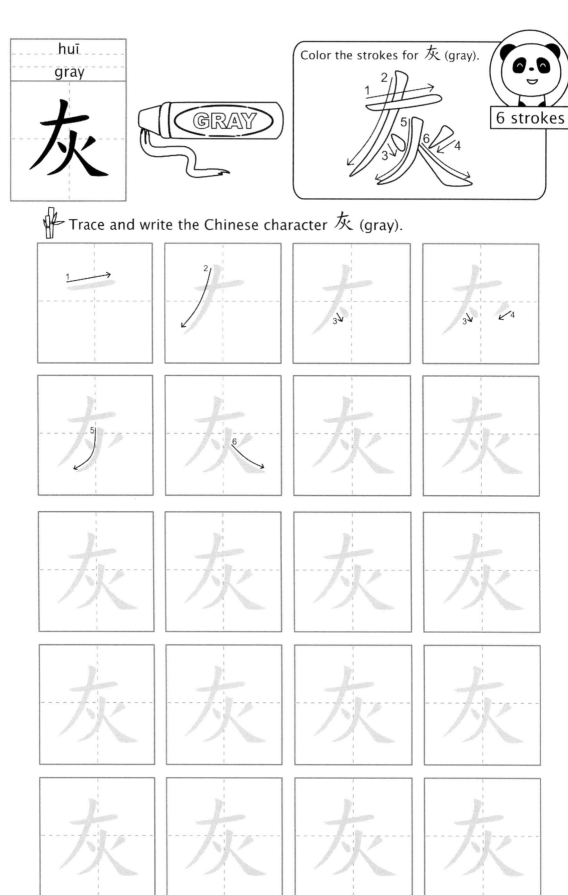

Write the missing stroke for 灰 on each crayon from the panda 熊猫 to the bamboo 竹子.

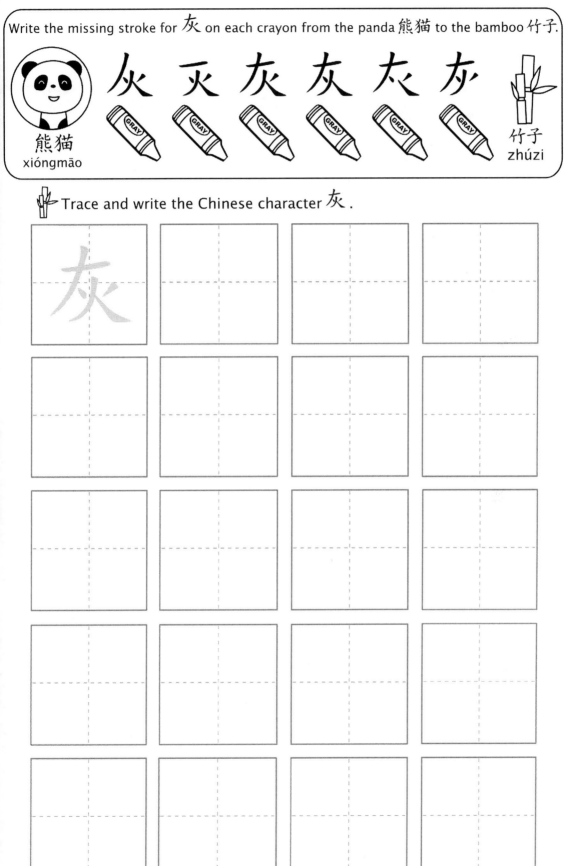

熊猫
xióngmāo

灰 灭 灰 灰 灰 灰

竹子
zhúzi

Trace and write the Chinese character 灰.

Good Job!

Practice writing characters you have learned below.

Good Job!

Practice writing characters you have learned below.

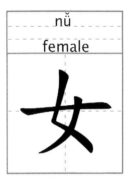

nǚ

female

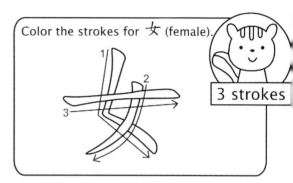

Trace and write the Chinese character 女 (female).

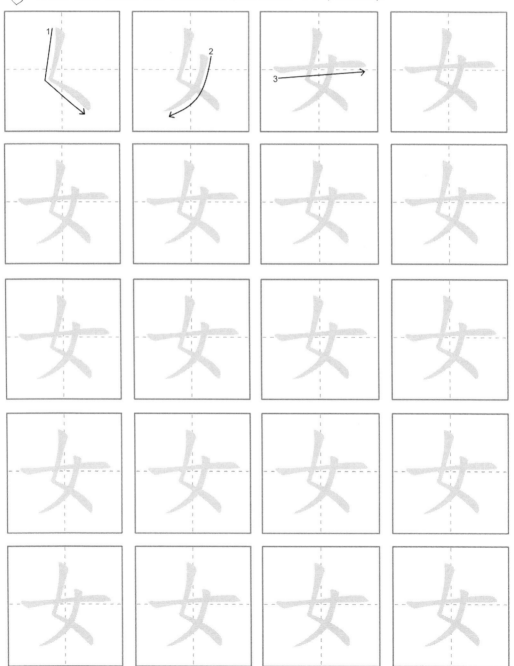

Write the missing stroke for 女 for each woman from the squirrel 松鼠 to the acorn 橡子.

ナ 七 女 女 ナ 七 女

松鼠
sōngshǔ

橡子
xiàng zi

Trace and write the Chinese character 女.

zi
child

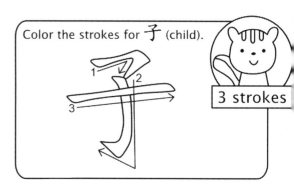

3 strokes

Trace and write the Chinese character 子 (child).

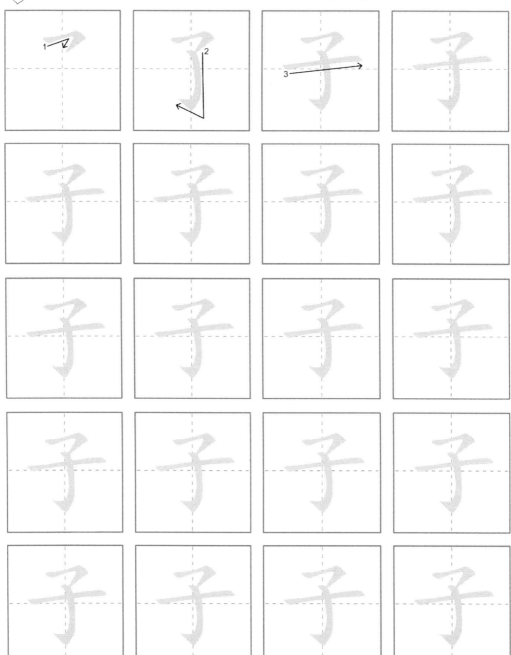

Write the missing stroke for 子 for each child from the squirrel 松鼠 to the acorn 橡子.

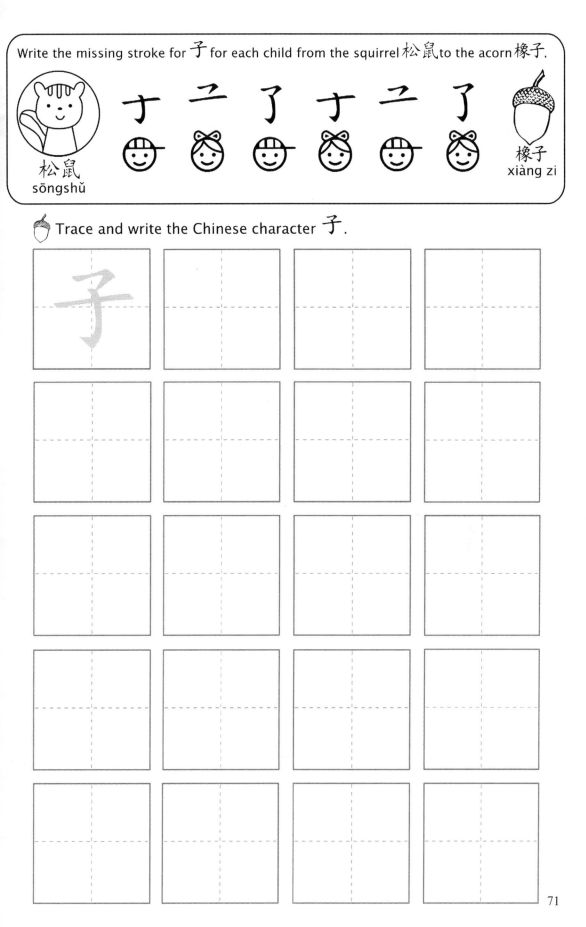

松鼠
sōngshǔ

橡子
xiàng zi

Trace and write the Chinese character 子.

hǎo
good

好

GOOD JOB!

Color the strokes for 好 (good).

1
好
3
2 4
6 5

6 strokes

Trace and write the Chinese character 好 (good).

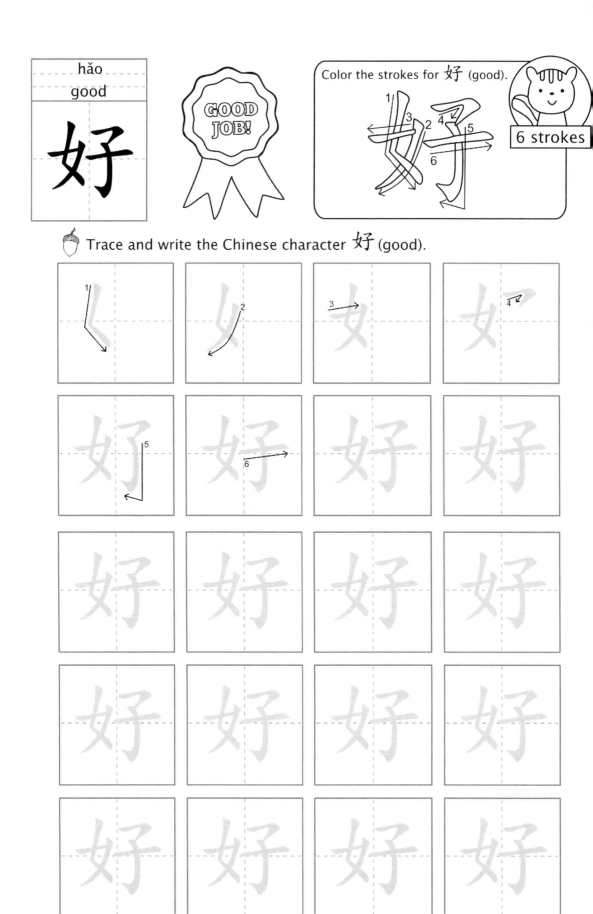

Write the missing stroke for 好 in each award from the squirrel 松鼠 to the acorn 橡子.

松鼠
sōngshǔ

孖 · 好 · 好 · 好 · 妇 · 奶

橡子
xiàng zi

Trace and write the Chinese character 好.

好

yè

page

页

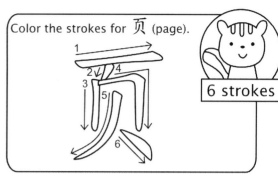

Color the strokes for 页 (page).

6 strokes

🌰 Trace and write the Chinese character 页 (page).

Write the missing stroke for 页 on each page from the squirrel 松鼠 to the acorn 橡子.

松鼠
sōngshǔ

橡子
xiàng zi

Trace and write the Chinese character 页 .

wèn

ask

问

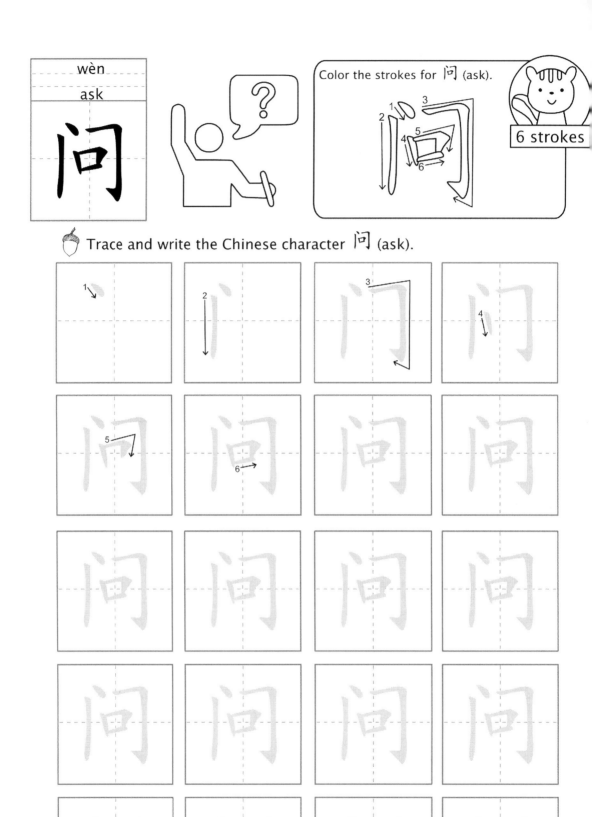

Color the strokes for 问 (ask).

6 strokes

🌰 Trace and write the Chinese character 问 (ask).

76

Write the missing stroke for 问 on each bubble from the squirrel 松鼠 to the acorn 橡子.

松鼠
sōngshǔ

问　司　卩　问　问　问

?　?　?　?　?　?

橡子
xiàng zi

Trace and write the Chinese character 问.

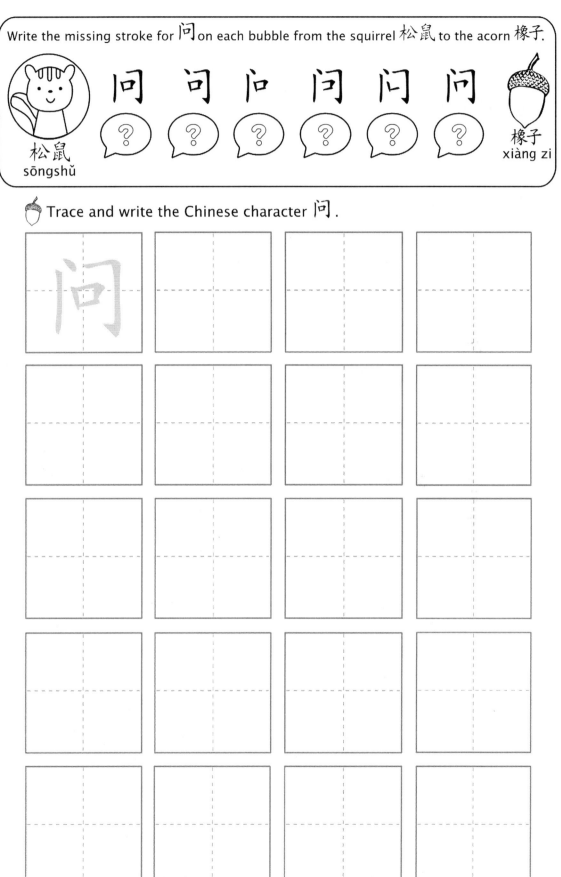

zhī
juice

汁

Color the strokes for 汁 (juice).

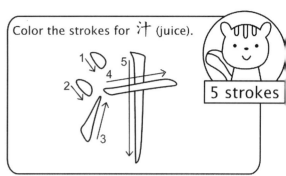

5 strokes

Trace and write the Chinese character 汁 (juice).

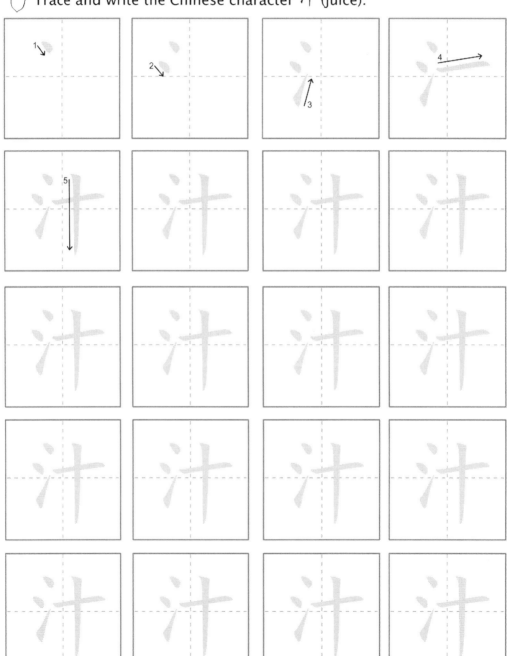

Write the missing stroke for 汁 on each juice box from the squirrel 松鼠 to the acorn 橡子.

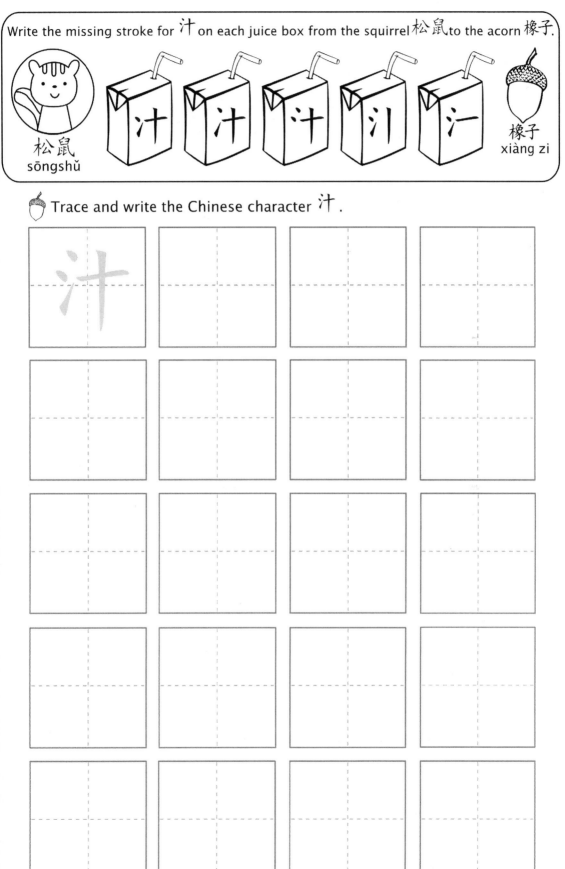

松鼠
sōngshǔ

橡子
xiàng zi

Trace and write the Chinese character 汁.

bù		
no, not		

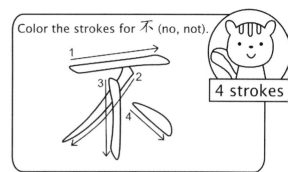

Color the strokes for 不 (no, not).

4 strokes

🌰 Trace and write the Chinese character 不 (no, not).

Write the missing stroke for 不 on the signs from the squirrel 松鼠 to the acorn 橡子.

松鼠
sōngshǔ

橡子
xiàng zi

Trace and write the Chinese character 不.

lěng
cold

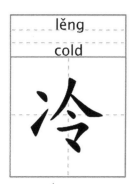

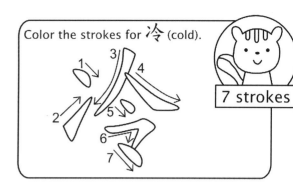

7 strokes

🌰 Trace and write the Chinese character 冷 (cold).

Write the missing stroke for 冷 on each therometer from the squirrel 松鼠 to the acorn 橡子.

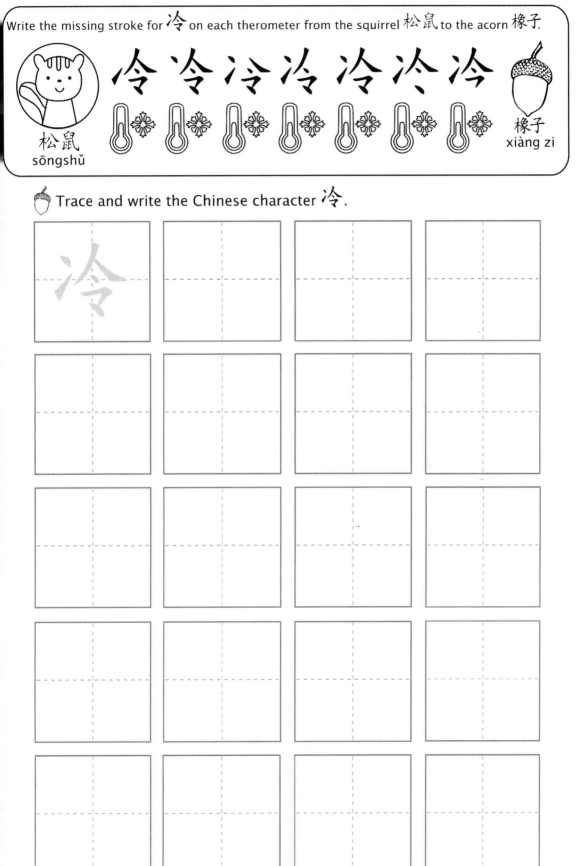

松鼠
sōngshǔ

冷 冷 冷 冷 冷 冷 冷

橡子
xiàng zi

Trace and write the Chinese character 冷.

dōng
winter

冬

Color the strokes for 冬 (winter).

5 strokes

🌰 Trace and write the Chinese character 冬 (winter).

Write the missing stroke for 冬 on each snowflakes from the squirrel 松鼠 to the acorn 橡子.

松鼠
sōngshǔ

冬　冬　冬　冬　冬

橡子
xiàng zi

Trace and write the Chinese character 冬.

fēng
wind

风

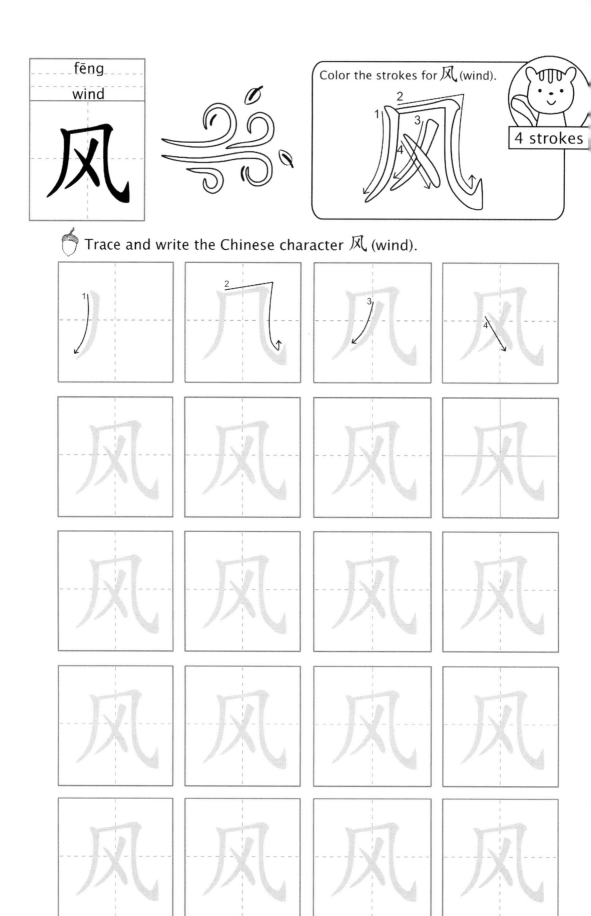

Color the strokes for 风 (wind).

4 strokes

🌰 Trace and write the Chinese character 风 (wind).

Write the missing stroke for 风 on the winds from the squirrel 松鼠 to the acorn 橡子.

松鼠
sōngshǔ

橡子
xiàng zi

Trace and write the Chinese character 风.

Good Job!

Practice writing characters you have learned below.

Good Job!

Practice writing characters you have learned below.

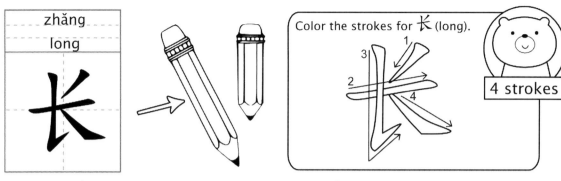

zhǎng

long

长

Color the strokes for 长 (long).

4 strokes

🐝 Trace and write the Chinese character 长 (long).

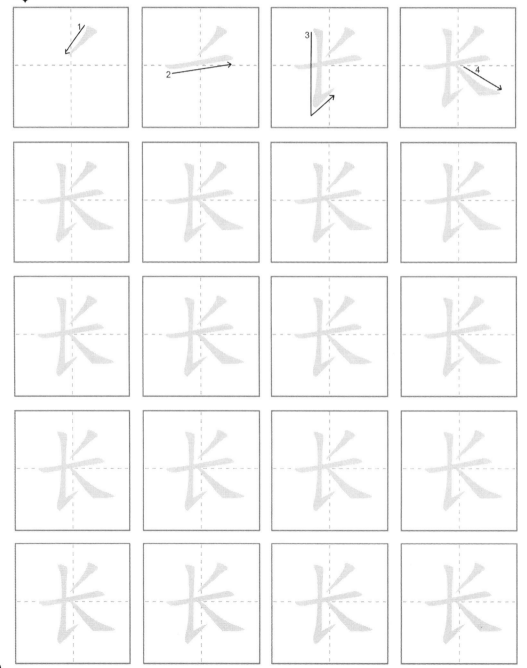

Write the missing stroke for 长 on the pencils from the bear 熊 to the honey 蜜糖 .

熊
xióng

蜜糖
mì táng

🐝 Trace and write the Chinese character 长 .

lóng
dragon

龙

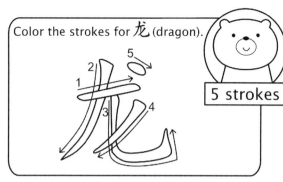

5 strokes

Trace and write the Chinese character 龙 (dragon).

92

Write the missing stroke for 龙 on the dragons from the bear 熊 to the honey 蜜糖.

熊
xióng

龙 屯 尤 尤 龙

蜜糖
mì táng

🐝 Trace and write the Chinese character 龙.

| hào |
| number |

号

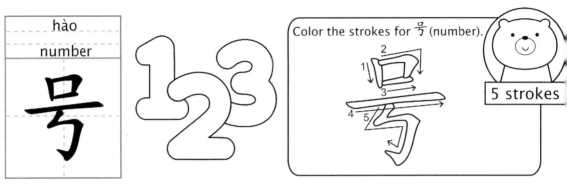

🐝 Trace and write the Chinese character 号 (number).

Write the missing stroke for 号 on the numbers from the bear 熊 to the honey 蜜糖.

熊
xióng

号　与　号　号　卩

蜜糖
mì táng

🐝 Trace and write the Chinese character 号.

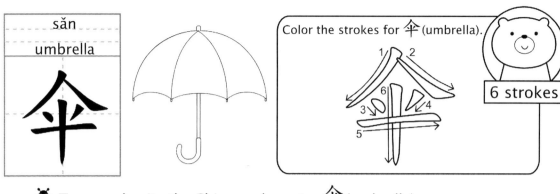

| sǎn |
| umbrella |

傘

Color the strokes for 傘 (umbrella).

6 strokes

🐝 Trace and write the Chinese character 傘 (umbrella).

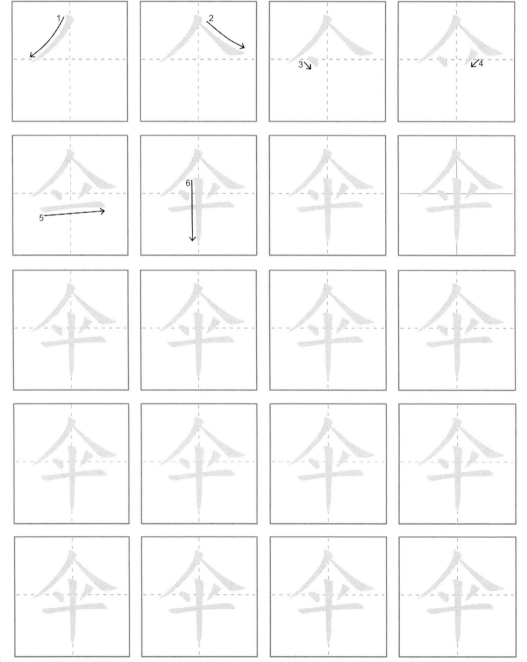

Write the missing stroke for 伞 on each umbrella from the bear 熊 to the honey 蜜糖.

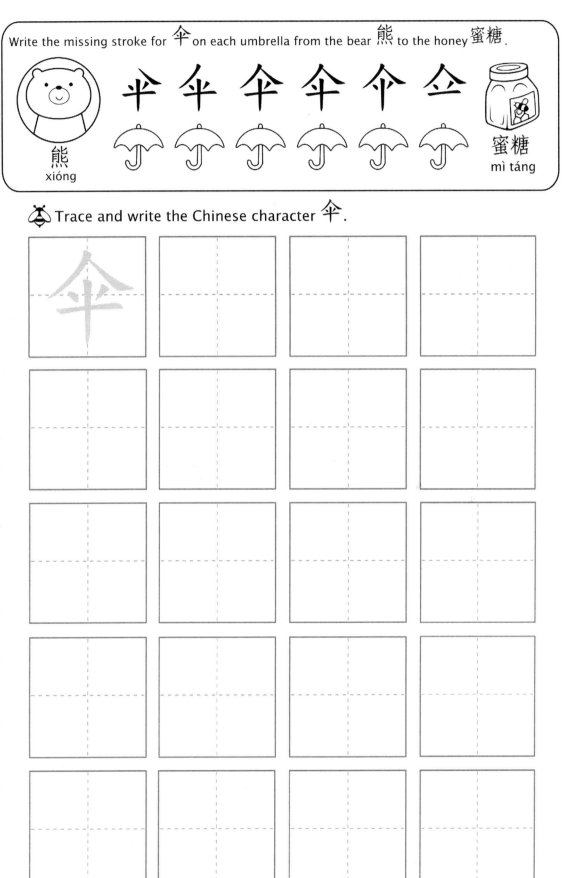

熊
xióng

伞 伞 伞 伞 伞 仝

蜜糖
mì táng

Trace and write the Chinese character 伞.

shí
stone

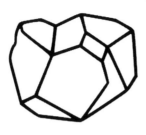

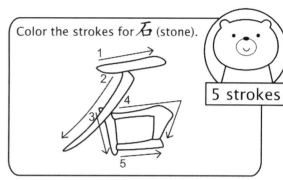

🐝 Trace and write the Chinese character 石 (stone).

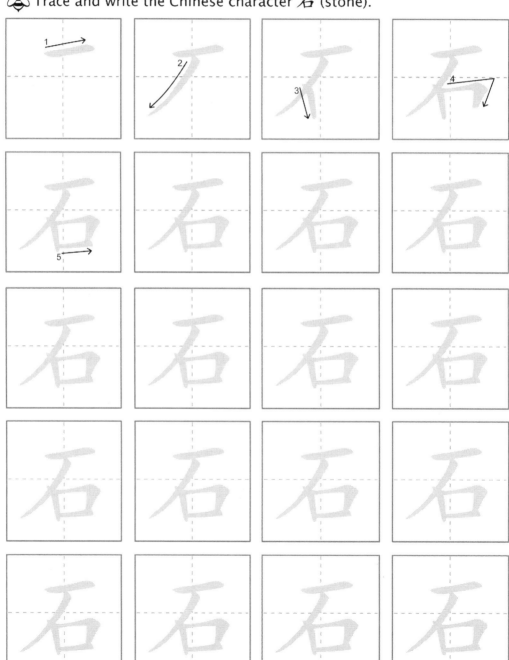

Write the missing stroke for 石 on each stone from the bear 熊 to the honey 蜜糖.

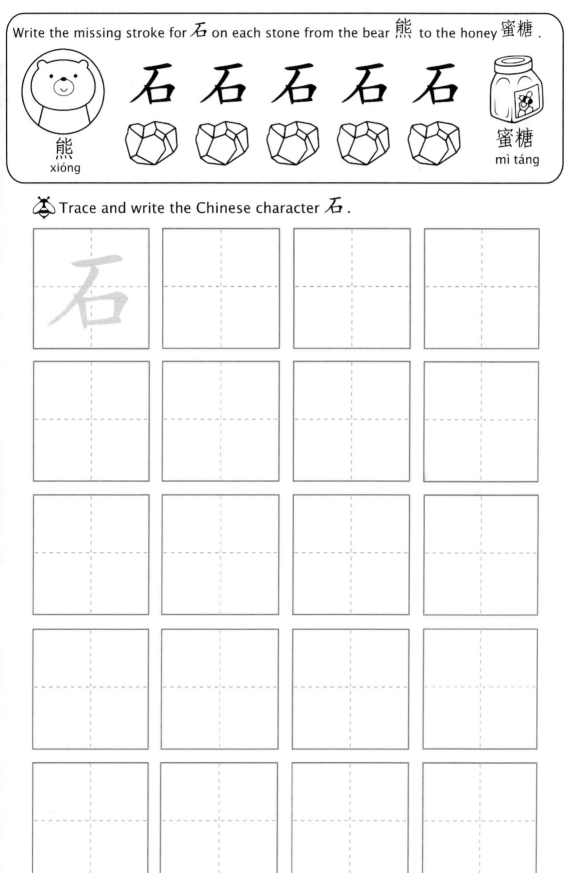

熊
xióng

石 石 石 石 石

蜜糖
mì táng

Trace and write the Chinese character 石.

| hàn |
| sweat |

汗

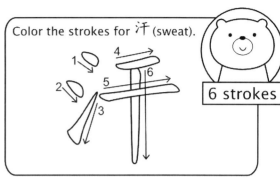

Color the strokes for 汗 (sweat).

6 strokes

🐝 Trace and write the Chinese character 汗 (sweat).

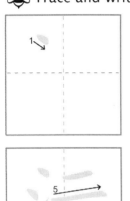 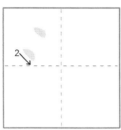 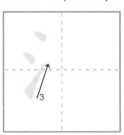 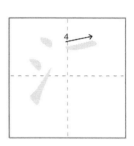

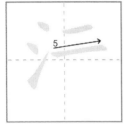   

 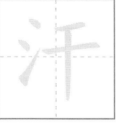  

  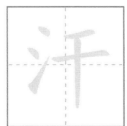 

Write the missing stroke for 汗 in each head from the bear 熊 to the honey 蜜糖.

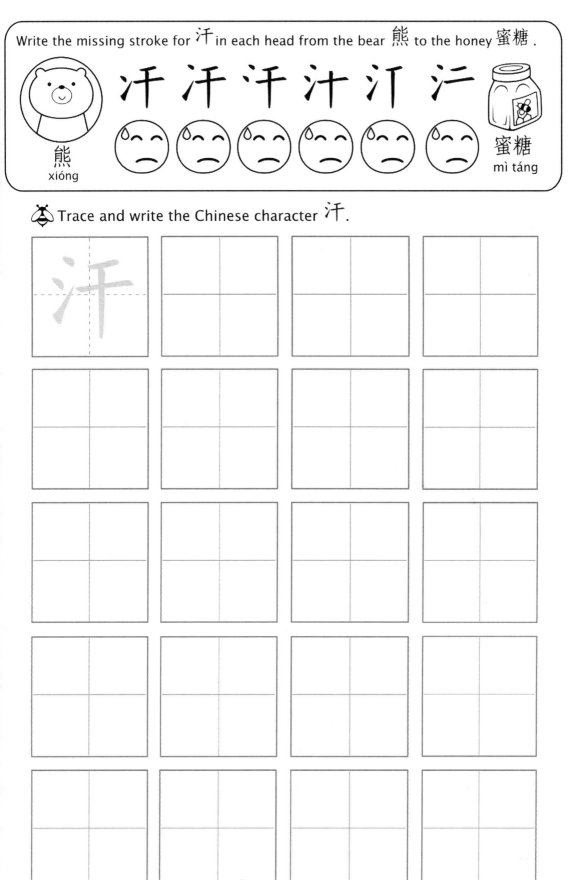

熊
xióng

汗 汗 汗 汁 汀 氵

蜜糖
mì táng

Trace and write the Chinese character 汗.

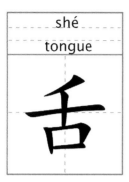

shé

tongue

Color the strokes for 舌 (tongue).

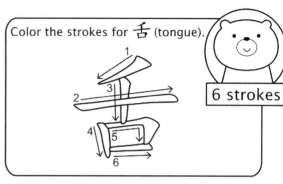

6 strokes

Trace and write the Chinese character 舌 (tongue).

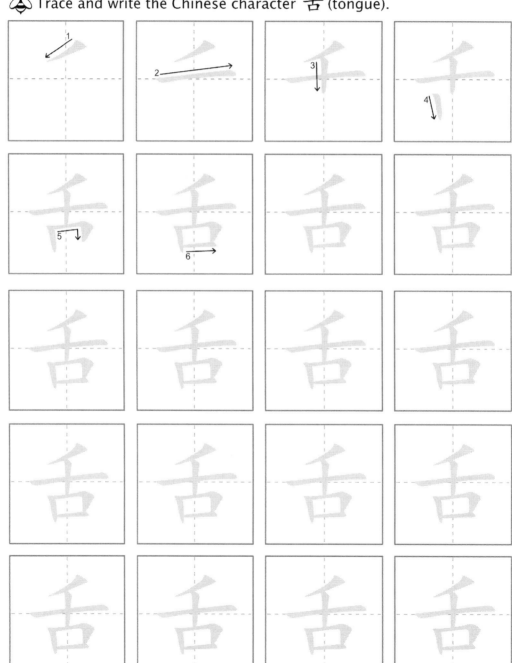

102

Write the missing stroke for 舌 on each tongue from the bear 熊 to the honey 蜜糖.

熊
xióng

古 舌 台 舌 舌 舌

蜜糖
mì táng

Trace and write the Chinese character 舌.

duì	
correct	

对

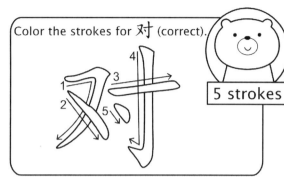

5 strokes

🐝 Trace and write the Chinese character 对 (correct).

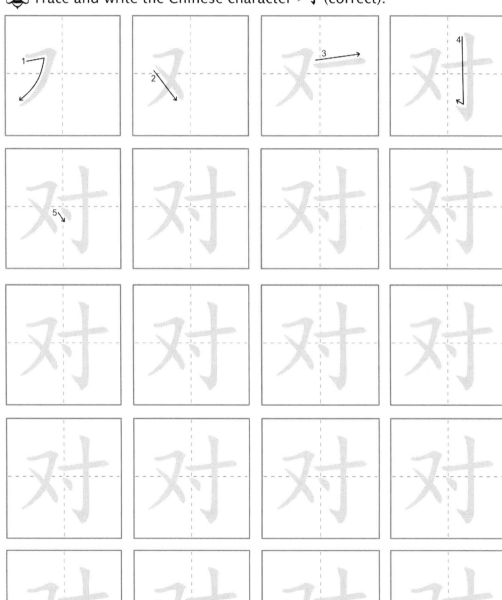

Write the missing stroke for 对 on each check mark from the bear 熊 to the honey 蜜糖.

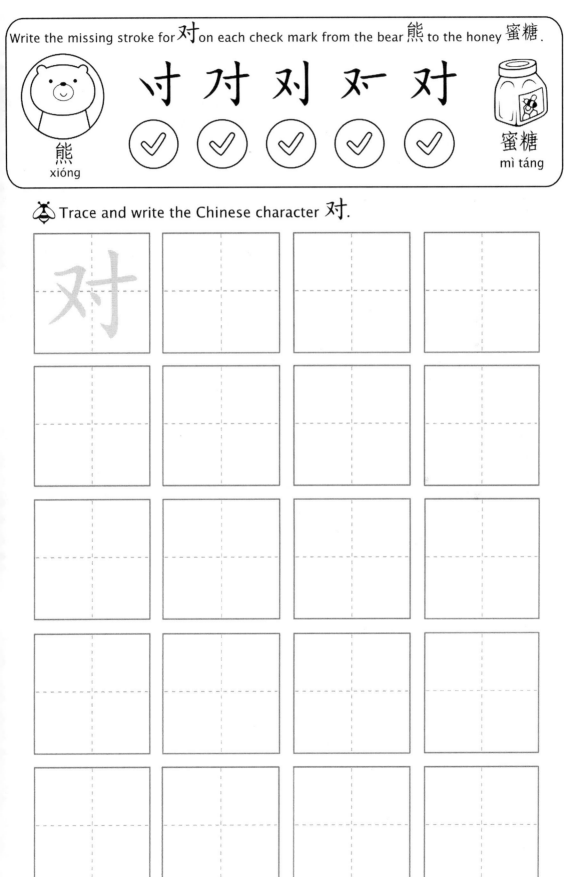

熊
xióng

对 对 对 对 对

蜜糖
mì táng

Trace and write the Chinese character 对.

mǎi
buy

买

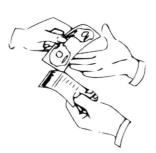

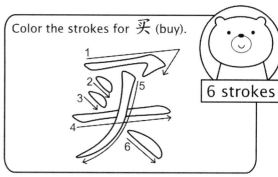

🐝 Trace and write the Chinese character 买 (buy).

Write the missing stroke for 买 on the bags from the bear 熊 to the honey 蜜糖.

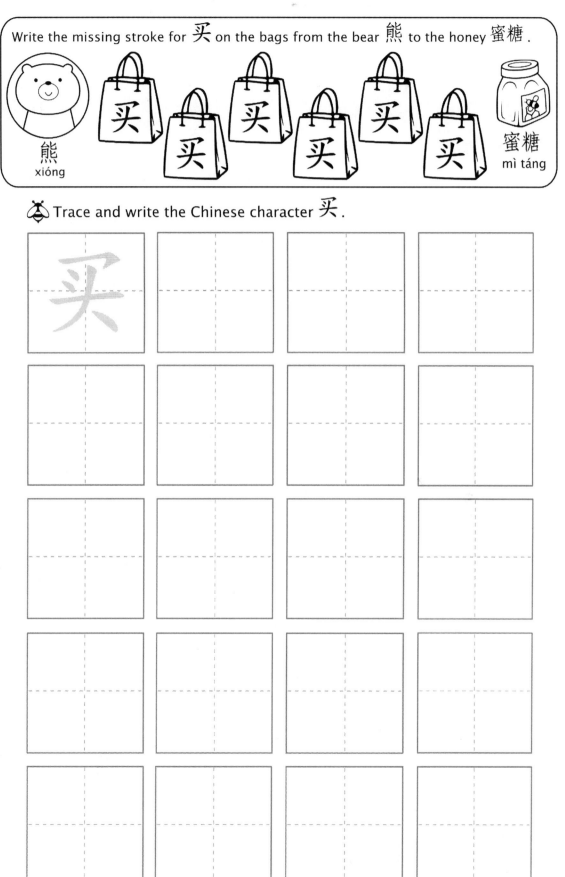

熊
xióng

蜜糖
mì táng

🐝 Trace and write the Chinese character 买.

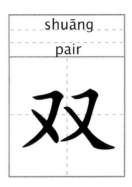

shuāng

pair

双

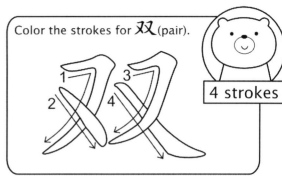

4 strokes

🐝 Trace and write the Chinese character 双 (pair).

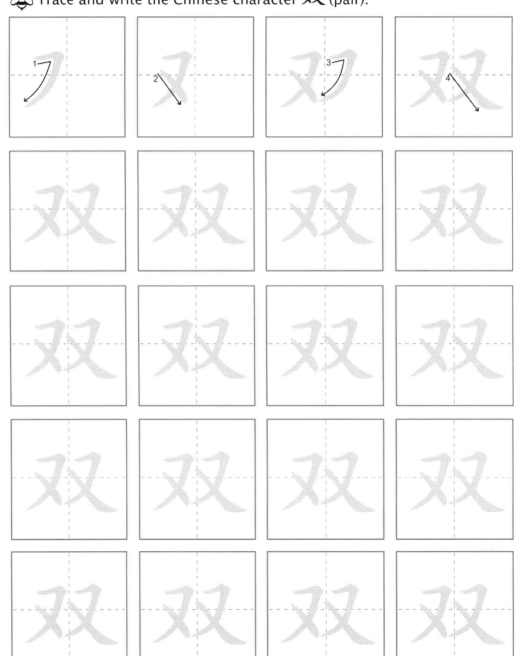

108

Write the missing stroke for 双 on the pairs of socks from the bear 熊 to the honey 蜜糖.

熊
xióng

双　双　又　双

蜜糖
mì táng

🐝 Trace and write the Chinese character 双.

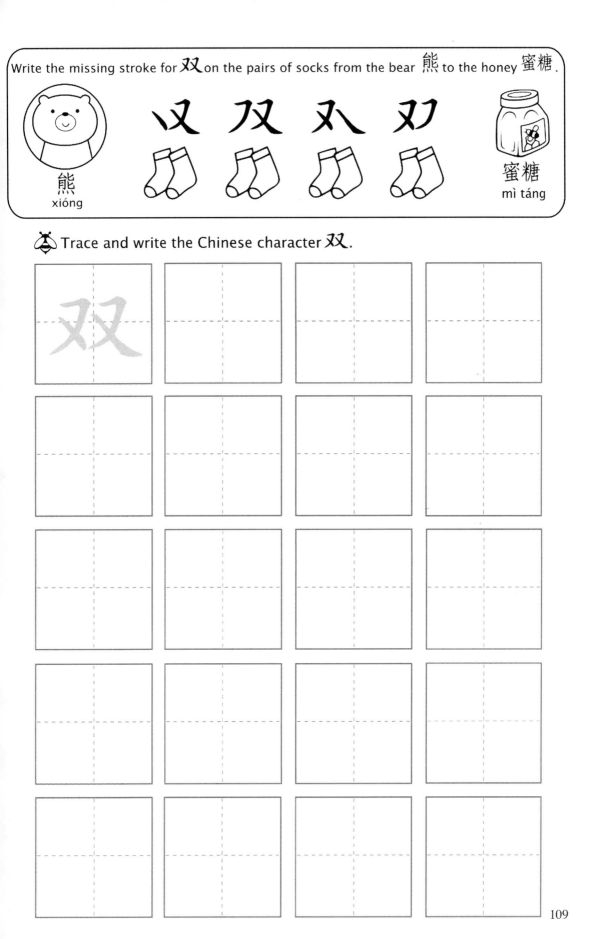

Good Job!

Practice writing characters you have learned below.

Good Job!

🐝 Practice writing characters you have learned below.

Made in the USA
San Bernardino,
CA